Revolution of Love

REVOLUTION OF LOVE

*The Canadian Revival
1971-72:*
Its Impetus and Theology

K. NEILL FOSTER
Foreword by Bill McLeod

HORIZON BOOKS
CAMP HILL, PENNSYLVANIA

Horizon Books
3825 Hartzdale Drive, Camp Hill, PA 17011

ISBN: 0-88965-140-X

© 1973, 1997 Horizon Books

All rights reserved
Printed in the United States of America

Dedication

To Carmelo Terranova, the Argentine Bible teacher who came eight thousand miles to teach us how to love, and to Asterio Wee, Juan Talion, Domingo Ferrer, Ismael de la Peña and hundreds of other Filipinos among whom and with whom we experienced the revolution of love.

Foreword

In a unique and powerful way Neill Foster has grasped clearly the essence of revival. To so many, revival has to do with subjective experiences of various kinds. To others it is questioned unless there are large numbers of people converted to Christ. To some the excitement generated by a true moving of God becomes the essence of revival.

There have been a number of powerful revivals in the Solomon Islands, though they do not call them that. They speak instead of "the falling of love." This book follows suit. *Revolution of Love* shows in a wonderful way that love is the true hallmark of genuine revival.

Spurgeon loved to quote this verse:

Praising God with all my might;
In the sea of God's delight,
Self is drowned, and I am free!
Christ and love remain in me.

You will find this book challenging and life changing. There are scores of examples of people who were blessed by the Holy Spirit and filled with the love of God in a soul-transforming way. They were, in a very real sense, revolutionized by love.

>   Rev. Bill McLeod,
>   Canadian Revival Fellowship

Contents

Chapter	Page
Introduction	11
1. Revolutionary Love	13
2. God Lives in Saskatchewan	15
3. The Roots of Revival	18
4. Sixty Million Times	25
5. Hunted by Conviction	29
6. The Lid Comes Off	35
7. Love Is Something You Do	38
8. To Your Neighbors	48
9. And to Your Enemies	54
10. Observable Love	57
11. That Bad Dog	63
12. The Chariot Has Brakes	69
13. The Logic of Love	73
14. The Fulness of Love	83
15. Exploding Love	88

Introduction

"Have you heard about the revival in Canada?"

This was the question put to me by pastor friends who met me in the Vancouver International Airport. The date was November, 1971 and I had just returned from an evangelistic and Bible teaching ministry in Mexico and Guatemala.

Of course I had not heard about revival in Canada, but I was interested and just a little bit uneasy.

I continued my journey toward the Peace Country of Alberta, where we make our home. In a second airport, the bustling frontier terminal at Fort St. John, B.C., I was again confronted by another pastor, "Have you heard about the revival in Saskatoon?"

By then I had. And the uneasiness was changing to just a little fear. I was not afraid of revival, but I was afraid of its spiritual and national significance. In Manchuria, Korea, and China, and to say nothing of Eastern Europe just before World War II, revivals had immediately preceded national and political disaster. What did all this mean for my wife, our children, our nation?

At home in Beaverlodge I discovered my wife as excited as everyone else about what God was doing in Saskatchewan. She had been talking to

Lou Sutera on the phone and was brimming with details.

Revival had come to Canada, and—as I was soon to find out—it was a revival of love. How it came to my own heart and what we have learned I shall relate as we proceed in these pages.

My object in writing is not to create a chronological account, nor even to trace a geographical pattern of the Holy Spirit's working. From incidents in the Philippines, in Saskatchewan, in Africa, from eternal truths made personal and alive I have drawn the raw materials. Thus, with a cautious mixture of narrative, scripture and experience I am seeking to describe the revolution of love—and to create a deep hunger in thousands of hearts for God's exploding love.

CHAPTER 1
Revolutionary Love

Love explodes in the congregation!
It is convulsed by the Holy Spirit!
This is the revolution of love!

These are strange new terms in the Christian vocabulary. Let us attempt an explanation of them by illustration.

In June of 1972 a revival team visited the Labason Evangelical Church on the Island of Mindanao, Republic of the Philippines. The telegram we had sent to announce our coming had not arrived. Besides, the Vacation Bible School was in progress.

But never mind, there would be a service, the pastor decided. The building itself was ample in size but unfinished. A dirt floor. Cement blocks for a platform and altar. Open windows. Lanterns in the evening. Still, on brief notice, the people came. And their hearts were hungry.

The revival team shared, each relating with deep honesty just how the Holy Spirit had dealt with him. An invitation was given.

Many of the believers moved forward to the altar, some began to weep, confessions were made to God and one another and Christian love began to be expressed.

Words fail, but a kind of divine epidemic had

been unleashed. A holy convulsion was cleansing the church.

Remarkably enough, in a second service in the same church a few days later, there was a further purging and if possible, a greater outpouring of love.

Undeniable revival.

Transparent honesty.

And love, such love.

The theme song of the revival team that visited Labason was strikingly appropriate. Composed earlier by the Daniebelle singers during a World Vision evangelistic crusade in Zamboanga, its lilting melody and powerful words proved a catalyst for revival wherever the teams went, first in Mindanao and later in the island of Luzon.

"Oh, there's a revolution of love in Labason,
You can feel the Spirit moving in the air,
There's a revolution of love in Labason
See the smiling happy faces everywhere.
Oh, I love you, my brother and my sister,
If you listen you can hear the people say:
There's a revolution of love in Labason
And you can join the revolution today."

What we want to share with you is incredibly exciting, but to begin we will have to go back a little.

CHAPTER 2
God Lives in Saskatchewan

In October of 1971 the Rev. William McLeod of Saskatoon, Saskatchewan, had scheduled an evangelistic crusade in his church with the Sutera Twins, Ralph and Lou, of Mansfield, Ohio. It might have been an ordinary campaign or even an extraordinary one since the Suteras were experienced evangelists who had travelled widely over the years and had consistently demonstrated the evangelistic gift.

But in a pattern which we shall discuss later, God began to do something very unusual in Saskatoon. The Ebenezer Baptist Church in Saskatoon was soon filled to capacity—and most important, key members of that same church began to be reconciled with one another. Two brothers who had not sung together for ten years and had not spoken for two years were reconciled. Love flowed like a river. And the fire burned.

In need of larger quarters, the meetings were moved to an Anglican church which in turn proved unable to hold the crowds. Then in an unprecedented move, Pastor Walter Boldt of the University Drive Alliance church cancelled his missionary convention in order not to stifle what God was doing and wanted to do in Saskatoon. Use of the large sanctuary at University Drive, seating eight hundred, was offered to the Baptists. And they accepted.

Pastor Boldt himself took an obscure seat in the balcony, and as he later confessed, critically watched the service unfold. The song service in his opinion was sub-normal. The movement of the service clumsy and inelegant. Previously he had wondered, why had God sent the revival to the Baptists and not University Drive? After all, he had reasoned, we are the largest evangelical church. We have the people. We have the prestige.

Suddenly, as Paster Boldt related later, God came upon that service. It was taken over by the Holy Spirit of Almighty God and everyone knew it. When the invitation to get right with God was given many believers and some unconverted responded to the appeal. Pastor Boldt sensed the Holy Spirit saying "You need to go to that altar." He did not go then, but when the call for counsellors was made, he went—but not to counsel. He went to get right with God himself.

The revival continued to grow until thousands were attending, hundreds were finding Christ and many, many lukewarm Christians were getting right with God.

The story of how the revival spread to Regina and later to the Okanagan in the interior of British Columbia will probably be written by others at the appropriate time.

We were not in any of the meetings in Saskatoon. But something was in the air in Western Canada. And if the general populace did not sense anything unusual, those with spiritual discernment certainly did. There was, in the words of one, "an incredible sense of destiny" upon the evangelicals in Western Canada.

Our first-hand introduction to the revival was in the Okanagan, scenic fruit valley of British Columbia. About one thousand people were gathered in a public hall in Kelowna. Lou Sutera was the preacher but because of the length of the service I could not stay long enough to hear him preach.

Still, though no one told me it was revival, suddenly I sensed that it was. The suddenness of the realization shocked me. And for the first time in my ministry I knew that revival was distinct—it was not evangelism though it was evangelistic; it was not blessing though it was blessed. It was a fire—ignited by God among people who had for years been evangelized and blessed.

CHAPTER 3

The Roots of Revival

The spreading of the revival was a religious phenomenon. Nothing like it had ever happened in Western Canada. Especially used were revival teams of laymen and women who had met God in a new way. They went out to share, many times telling others in brokenness and tears what God had done for them. Ribbons of asphalt across the broad prairies had indeed paved the way for rapid communication. If you like, the phenomenon of the phenomenon was lay participation.

That laymen were allowed to participate at all was a vitally important factor in what transpired. A major key. The preachers stepped aside to allow the Holy Spirit to control the services. And the Holy Spirit spoke very powerfully through the inspired testimonies of the people.

And conversely, whenever the preachers refused to surrender control of the pulpit or service to the Holy Spirit there was no revival. (This is not to suggest that services were uncontrolled or that the pastors or evangelists allowed disorder; nor are we intimating that the importance of preaching and pastoral ministries was at all minimized.)

The first time I personally witnessed the surrender of a service to the Spirit's control was in Penticton, British Columbia. A number of men had gathered to share. As the spontaneous testimonies were given a discernible pattern developed. In various ways the men from different denominational backgrounds kept saying the same thing, "God heals."

From time to time one of the men would kneel at a chair in the center of the room asking for prayer. Though we did not know it at the time, there was a man there with an incurable disease. And he stepped forward asking for prayer. Medical testimony later confirmed a most unusual healing.

But God was not talking to me about healing. For me there was just one inescapable impression. "We preachers have been in the way, we have been obstructing God's Spirit." The Holy Spirit, we discovered, is well able to control and guide a service if it is surrendered to Him.

The evangelical media also took note. *Christianity Today* observed that the revival was "intense but not charismatic." Sherwood Wirt of *Decision* did an imaginative article on revival in Winnipeg. *The Inquirer* out of Toronto also spread the news. The *Alliance Witness* from New York also gave solid, appreciative coverage. And in our own *Communicate* the revival was followed carefully.

Thousands of copies of the tract *Revival in Saskatoon* went around the world from the Western Tract Mission of that city, but that too is a story in itself. We are interested in the roots of the revival. How did it start?

Obviously of course it started in the heart of

God. There is no other explanation. But there are human factors—instruments, events and people—that God used.

Two years earlier, in 1969, the Rev. Duncan Campbell, a Presbyterian revivalist and God's instrument in the Hebrides revival, had visited Canada. In his extensive tour he visited many parts of the nation and it became his conviction at that time that Canada would be the next nation to experience revival. Privately and prophetically he had declared, "I believe the revival will begin in the Ebenezer Baptist Church in Saskatoon."

How right he was!

The roots of the revival were varied. Something was happening among the young people and it had been going on for two years or more. Many conferences, camps and retreats reported unusual movings of the Holy Spirit.

In our own camping program at Nakamun, about 60 miles northwest of Edmonton, Alberta, it certainly was so. Both 1970 and 1971 were years of most unusual blessing among the teenagers. Burning devotion. Fervent love. Really, revival had in one sense already come to the youth, though the eyes of their elders were unseeing.

The Bible school movement of Western Canada is distinct in Church history. Great schools like the Prairie Bible Institute, the Briercrest Bible Institute, the Winnipeg Bible College, the Canadian Bible College and the Berean Bible College, along with other institutions, had graduated over the years literally thousands of young people, not all of whom made their way to the "ends of the earth." If there are two million evangelicals in Canada, fully a quarter of them probably live in the sparsely populated western provinces of Canada. If you like, a Bible belt, and fertile ground for a spiritual awakening.

The Mennonite influence in Western Canada is also considerable. Though they are divided into several groups, one thing is especially true—their denominational history is one of revivals. A large percentage of the membership of all evangelical churches in Western Canada comes from a Mennonite background. These people, though many times no longer worshipping in the church of their heritage, were still revivalistic by tradition and especially responsive to the awakening. And willing to give it massive supoort. We should not be surprised that revival began in Saskatoon, a city of strong Mennonite traditions.

Dr. Bill Bright and the Campus Crusade for Christ were also having increasing impact in Canada. Hundreds of people were attending the lay institutes, learning how to share their faith, how to experience the abundant life and appropriate the fullness of the Holy Spirit. As the saying goes, people were being "turned on." Since revival has come we now realize that some were being revived even then.

The same can be said for Mr. Bill Gothard and his Institute in Basic Youth Conflicts. In meetings advertised only by word of mouth, thousands were attending seminars conducted not by an evangelist but a Bible teacher. Revolutionary truths about conscience, fasting and other basic Bible concepts were being communicated to masses. In recent years these large gatherings have been held only in the United States, but Canadians were attending. And, we realize now, being revived.

Also more localized revivals through the ministry of the Sutera Twins had occurred in Abbotsford and Prince George, British Columbia. Revival had come to the Abbotsford Alliance Church and Rev. M. Johnson first. Then two years later, in 1971, the Prince George Evangelical Free Church where Rev. C. Dietrick is the pastor was revived. By Pastor Dietrick's own appraisal, ninety percent of the church was renewed.

A revival team of lay people from Abbotsford had come to Prince George to share and they had sparked revival there. Later, people from Prince George were to go 800 miles to Saskatoon to share. Most important, Pastor Dietrick had carried for one year a most unusual prayer-burden for revival. It was not till the middle of the Prince George meetings that the intense burden lifted and he was able to sleep normally again.

And then there was Nakamun. In 1971, the Suteras had been evening evangelists at the ninth annual Nakamun Family Camp. It was a most unusual camp. The Rev. Paul Kenyon of Sandusky, Ohio, and the Rev. Carmelo Terranova of Buenos Aires completed the ministering team. God was pleased to especially bless Mr. Terranova's ministry in an unusual way. In other years there had always been a high point, a climax in each camp. But in 1971 there was one—and another—and a third.

It was on the last of these occasions that divine love was poured out. The only way to explain it is to say that God's love just rolled out over the camp grounds. Many of us were irrevocably and forever changed. My wife was inexplicably different. It was not until revival came later that I realized what had happened to her at camp.

Since we have been so vitally connected to Nakamun (Family Camp director for ten years now) I have hesitated to suggest that even one of the roots of the revival might have been at Nakamun. But in recent ministry in the Philippines where I saw for the first time in my own ministry that which was undeniably revival, I could not deny that one of the roots went down to Nakamun. If anything, it was the love root.

We like what Ralph and Lou themselves say concerning the beginning of the revival.

"Could it have begun in the heart of the late Duncan Campbell who told Canadian audiences how God had shown him the entire Dominion of Canada in flames of revival fire? Could it have been in the testimony of lay people sharing their faith with others in Prince George, British Columbia? Could it have been in the heart of the Prince George pastor who could not sleep normally for one year because of prayer-burden for revival? Could it have been in the heart of the British Columbia woman who has been praying for four years that God would use our ministry for revival? Could it have been in the heart of the Saskatoon pastor who could do nothing but pray in his study for several months before the revival came? Could it have been in the step of faith exercised by pastor and people of another Saskatoon church to cancel a missionary convention and become part of what God was doing? We may have to wait until we get to heaven to be able to know the real answer. But meantime, to God be the glory!" [1]

Speaking about the origins of revival, the Rev.

---

[1] Ralph and Lou Sutera, Revival Fellowship News, Regina, July, 1972, p. 2.

Armin R. Gesswein, Lutheran revivalist, had this to say: "Revival begins when hidden springs, that are not able to be traced, break forth."[2] The words fit exceptionally well when applied to the awakening in Canada.

And I must return to say what I said a few pages earlier, revival began in God's heart of love.

---

[2] Sermon, Armin R. Gesswein, September 14, 1972.

CHAPTER 4
Sixty Million Times

"God loves me. God loves me. I've heard that sixty million times." That was the response of one brother who was faced with the basic truth of this chapter. But he stayed to hear more.

Before I go further and tell you how revival came to my own heart, there is an absolutely vital concept which must be introduced here.

God loves you. God loves me. These simple words wait to be understood. When they finally are understood the concept which they embody becomes the hinge upon which the spiritual phenomenon we call revival moves.

As he passed lonely hours shepherding farm machines over hundreds of northern Canadian acres, my brother-in-law prayed an earnest prayer. "God, you love, I know. But how do you love me? Lord, show me." And God answered him.

"Cecil, you want to know how I love you? It is something like this. Chris, your infant son, has been sick, right? And you noticed how Normie reacted. Your wife was quite despondent while little Chris was in the hospital, she wandered aimlessly around the house, she couldn't eat, she nearly became sick herself. That's how much Normie loves little Chris. And my love is something like that."

When Cec related the story to me I had to agree

that it was a beautiful glimpse of human love, which in turn is a portrait of God's love. But we also know that is not a complete picture. The very immensity of God's great love makes it very difficult to describe.

At Ntorosso in Mali, West Africa, an African pastor approached me. Then in Bambara, through an interpreter, he told me his story. For many years he had preached the gospel. Now he was old but he still remembered the difficult days.

Yes, he remembered very well when they beat him for his faith in Yesu. But somehow, he said, the blows did not hurt. God protected him.

And as I listened to the animated conversation, gazed into his sparkling eyes and marvelled at the blackness of his skin contrasted against the long light brown tunic, I thought, "He was surrounded by love. That is why he was not hurt. Surrounded by love."

A mother's deep concern for a tiny red-headed baby passing through a crisis of life reveals something of God's love, as does the joyful account of a black man who has cheerfully accepted persecution for Christ's sake.

Still, our concept of God's love for us must remain terribly dwarfed until we read the words of Paul.

"Who then can ever keep Christ's love from us? When we have trouble or calamity, when we are hunted down or destroyed, is it because He doesn't love us any more? And if we are hungry, or penniless, or in danger, or threatened with death, has God deserted us?

"No, for the scriptures tell us that for His sake we must be ready to face death at every moment of the day—we are like sheep awaiting slaughter; but despite all this, overwhelming victory is ours through Christ who loved us enough to die for us.

"For I am convinced that nothing can ever separate us from His love. Death can't and life can't. The angels won't, and all the powers of hell itself cannot keep God's love away. Our fears for today, our worries about tomorrow, or where we are—high above the sky, or in the deepest ocean—nothing will ever be able to separate us from the love of God demonstrated by our Lord Jesus Christ when He died for us" (Romans 8:35-39, Living Bible).

God's love is focused on the cross.

These pages and thoughts have come to me in different parts of the world and many times I have had the feeling that the Holy Spirit was, in a special way, completing the message of this book.

There was that awareness when Urunu, a handsome young African pastor, came to me at Dedougou, Upper Volta. Hesitantly, he offered this exhortation: "Is the message of love really complete without the preaching of the cross?" There was an instant accord in my heart. "The preaching of the cross is to them that perish foolishness; but unto us which are saved it is the power of God" (I Corinthians 1:18).

Yes, God's love is focused on the cross. There the flame of God's love was ignited. Make no mistake, the preaching of love is the preaching of the cross. And the preaching of the cross is the preaching of love.

Love is like a protective flame. It comes from the heart of God and nothing can penetrate it, nothing can come between our hearts and this gentle flame of God's love.

Not a passing baby sickness—nor even a fatal one.

Not an African beating under knotted desert clubs.

Nor famine. Nor nakedness. Nor peril. Nor sword. Nor martyrdom. Death cannot penetrate the loving flame. Nothing in life can quench it. Not angels nor demons nor even satanic princes.

Time cannot dim it. Neither the light-years of heaven nor the innumerable fathoms of ocean trenches are able by any means to overwhelm it. God's love is supreme.

And it surrounds us all. It surrounds you. It surrounds me. Visualize yourself as wrapped, completely enveloped in this flaming robe of God's love.

There can be no really useful discussion of spiritual awakening nor even an effective testimony given apart from the recognition that all that has happened in Western Canada and many parts of the world really began in the loving heart of God, that Canada's revival was ignited by the fire of heavenly love.

If you like, you may consider this book a letter from one of God's children—joyously wrapped in love—to all the rest. God loves you, God loves you, God loves you. Sixty million times or so, the revolution of love begins right there.

CHAPTER 5
Hunted by Conviction

Now at this juncture I want to explain that God has done something new for me. I was converted as a boy of eight; there was a crisis experience of the filling of God's Holy Spirit in 1956, followed later by rewarding and fruitful pastorates in British Columbia. And for ten years I had been an evangelist. Except on very rare occasions there were always inquirers. And there were, thank God, more than a few miracles along the way—such as the one under the stars in Colombia when an 8-year-old girl put aside her crutches and walked beautifully.

God was blessing the evangelistic association, the writing ministry, our camps and our family. If you had told me that I needed to be revived I might have laughed at you.

But there was an uneasiness within too. A clutter of things little and big was gradually shorting the circuits of God's power.

Specifically, I had participated with five Christian businessmen in founding a business "for God." But the relationship bothered me. And in the beginning the business was not especially blest.

We had a conference planned for the Chateau Lacombe in Edmonton in November nineteen seventy-one. The theme was to be "Doing Business for God." I was about to propagate an idea on which I myself was wavering. It did not augur well for the Christian Conference on Business, as we called it.

Meanwhile, the revival was convulsing the evangelical churches of Saskatoon—and spreading fast. I wrote to Pastor Boldt who was scheduled to speak at the Edmonton conference in the Chateau. Would he, I wanted to know, bring some revived people to the conference?

Before he received my letter he phoned. "I don't want to talk about finance, I want to talk about revival." I agreed. And if I had not, he later told me, he had intended to cancel his ministry at the convention.

Conviction had been building in my heart for weeks. As I had hunted moose in the wilderness near our home I had cancelled the conference a thousand times in my mind. But a thousand and one times I had decided to go ahead. My wife's observation proved more accurate than I dreamed: "Either this conference is the biggest mistake we have ever made, or God is going to do something tremendous."

In the first service of the conference Walter Boldt told the Saskatoon story to about 25 business people and pastors. My heart was broken. I wept through nearly the entire hour as he shared. I had no idea what revival was, but instinctively I wanted it. I asked God to revive me, I told Him I'd go all the way, and I asked Him to make me a revivalist. Then some of the men gathered round, laid their hands gently upon me and prayed for me. Exactly what happened I could not tell. But something surely had. Soon the three-day conference was over, but surprisingly enough, the conviction I had sensed before, was, if anything, more acute.

Revival, I was discovering, was not just a blessing: it was as we say, a whole new ball game. As my wife and I drove the 300 miles home to the Peace River Country, we discussed the conference, and especially the phenomenon of conviction, spiritual experience and then intensified conviction.

Finally, as we drove along discussing and sharing what had happened at the Chateau Lacombe I came to realize that God was angry with me—that my motives were wrong. The business we had organized was set up so that all profits would be designated for Christian work. I had participated because I would be able to designate for *my* work for the Lord. I was more interested in *my* evangelistic association than I was in God's glory. A divided heart. So I brought that before the Lord and received His forgiveness.

But the conviction did not abate. I next found myself in ministry at Yarrow in the Fraser Valley of British Columbia. The church which I had helped found and had pastored for nearly three years had asked that I return for an evangelistic campaign. Mr. Jim Sellers, the gospel singer from Spokane, shared the ministry.

The meetings began slowly with not much open response, but Pastor Orlin Craig had received a promise, "The Lord whom ye seek shall come suddenly into His temple." We prayed and preached and waited.

Not that the Holy Spirit was inactive. He was talking to me. In prayer He made it very clear to me that revival was rolling in from the prairies.

In fact, it soon became painfully clear that revival was everywhere in that church except in one little spot—right behind the pulpit. If it was a vision it certainly did not need any interpretation. I knew who was behind the pulpit. I was. And God was saying, "You are the hindrance to revival here."

When God talks to you like that you get down to business. I said, "Lord, I won't preach again till all is clear. I can't." And rather determinedly, I retired to pray. (I just happened to know what the problem was!)

It was the tendency to get my hands into things they ought not to be in, illicit and obsessive love for business. And I recognized that it was of the flesh. And since for years I had preached the power of the cross for Christian living I knew what I needed to do. This manifestation of self had to be crucified.

Then the Lord gave me a scripture, "Likewise reckon ye also yourselves to be dead indeed unto sin, but alive unto God" (Romans 6:11).

But I did not like the verse. Old Agag was prancing and mincing, "Lord," I said, "this is not sin, it is just the self life." How subtle! Self is the essence of sin. The sin nature had to be dealt with.

Finally, I capitulated. "Lord, it is the sin nature. It has to die." Then deliberately, I said something like this, "Almighty God, in the name of Jesus Christ, I now crucify this tendency I have to get my hands into things in which they ought not to be, this illicit love of business. I crucify it by the Holy Spirit. In Jesus' name, Amen."

I was not expecting an experience. But there was one just the same. A beautiful peace swept over my soul. And though my hands were folded across my chest, my arms seemed to be spread out as if on the cross with Jesus, and my hands impaled there with His. And how meaningful the scripture became, "I am crucified with Christ; nevertheless I live; yet not I, but Christ liveth in me" (Galatians 2:20).

There was new power in the meetings after that. Two husbands who had resisted the claims of Christ when I was pastor, who had continued ten years in unbelief since we left, were among the inquirers.

The Holy Spirit moved deeply in the whole congregation. In a pronounced and obvious way, the Lord, whom we had sought, had come suddenly into His temple. All praise to God!

But the conviction lingered. There was more in my heart obstructing the Holy Spirit, although I did not know what it was. In fact, previously I had always scoffed at the suggestion that there might be anything in anyone's heart about which they did not know. But not anymore. "Thou . . . knowest not that thou art wretched, and miserable, and poor, and blind, and naked" (Revelation 3:17). There *are* things in our hearts unknown to us.

Finally, after about six weeks had elapsed since the first work of revival in my heart. I sensed that a turning point was coming.

One night as we were driving in a nearby city I said to my wife, "Wifey, I don't know where all this ends but one thing I *know*, the Lord *knows* I love Him."

The next day I drove toward Edmonton. Before the first hundred miles had clipped by, the Holy Spirit had spoken once more, "Your problem, my son, is that you don't love me with all your heart."

If there is such an experience as being revived, it happened to me in those six weeks. But God did not stop. There have been many more probings of the Spirit since—and as I see it now, all were necessary to bring the revolution of love to my heart.

CHAPTER 6

The Lid Comes Off

For years I have had a stock answer for a stock question.

Many times I heard, "There is something in my heart but I don't know what it is."

Assuming that the question was at least partly dishonest, my answer was always sarcastically the same, "Get down and guess a while."

But not any more.

There are things in our hearts that we do not realize. And only when the "lid" comes off do we discover what really stands between ourselves and the revolution of love which is revival.

Perhaps we could define the "lid" as a callousness that becomes a cover, deflecting the arrows of conscience and stifling the Holy Spirit.

Personally, I have had, over a number of years, what I deemed to be an unusually sensitive conscience, one that was easily capable of bringing me into bondage and morbid introspection. In my struggle to achieve spiritual balance, I had begun to accommodate certain sins and attitudes.

For example, there was a preacher with whom I was cool. I was careful not to speak against him or criticize him because I didn't want to have to go and apologize to him.

The cover was peeled off. "You don't really love

that brother, do you?" the Holy Spirit said to me. "I want you to go to him and ask forgiveness for an unloving attitude, for not loving him."

I promised the Lord I would do it and I did. To my surprise and delight he responded warmly and deeply. A relationship was healed. And I learned once again that we don't always know what is in our hearts. Of course, the Scriptures had made it clear long before.

The trespass offering in the Old Testament had an interesting function. "If a soul commit a trespass, and sin through ignorance... then he shall bring for his trespass... a ram without blemish" (Leviticus 5:15). It is clear that there was an Old Testament provision for unknown sins.

Psalm nineteen also reflects this truth, "But how can I ever know what sins are lurking in my heart? Cleanse me from these hidden faults" (vs. 12, Living Bible).

Other scriptures reinforce the thought. "Search me, O God, and know my heart: try me and know my thoughts: and *see it there be any wicked way in me*" (Psalm 139:23, 24). "You say, 'I am rich, with everything I want; I don't need a thing.' And you don't realize that spiritually you are wretched and miserable and poor and blind and naked" (Revelation 3:17, Living Bible).

A word of caution is in order here. If Satan cannot stop believers from opening themselves to the Holy Spirit and surrendering fully to Christ, he then may pounce upon the serious Christian, subtly mixing accusation with conviction and distorting the revival.

The best advice which can be given is that which an earnest laymen received from a wise

Mennonite pastor in the Fraser Valley of British Columbia. "Invite the Holy Spirit to search your heart and then ask the Lord not to allow a single accusation from the enemy to be added."

Still, it is worth repeating, the lid must come off and we must get honest with ourselves, with each other, and with God.

Pastor Les Hamm and the congregation of the Hillsdale Alliance Church in Regina, Saskatchewan, have experienced a remarkable and ongoing revival which also began in the fall of 1971. For Sherwood Wirt, editor of *Decision,* Pastor Hamm summed it up succinctly, "Revival is honesty and love."

The mask comes down and the lid comes off.

And as so many have said, "You can afford to be honest." Because honesty generates respect and love.

CHAPTER 7

Love Is Something You Do

What began to happen in Western Canada in the fall of 1971 was not an emotional orgy. Certainly there were emotions. And tearful, red eyes were right in style, but so were smiling, glowing faces.

As is always the case when God does something deep and genuine, what was happening was based firmly and squarely upon the Word of God.

There is one text that particularly focuses revival truth in a very few words: "Thou shalt love the Lord thy God with all thy heart, and with all thy soul, and with all thy mind, and with all thy strength: this is the first commandment" (Mark 12:30).

First of all, there is no escaping the obvious. It is a commandment, admittedly from the Old Testament, but reemphasized and reinforced, even amplified as we shall see, by Jesus. Moreover, the Saviour makes it clear once again that this commandment is the *first* one. If the Master put it first there can be no doubt about its importance. It obviously deserves the most attention from us and we are likely to find that its truth is foundational.

Also, commandments are to be obeyed. Not just read or discussed. The command is to *love*

God. There are other commands which evangelicals regularly obey such as the ones ordering all believers to be baptized and to be filled with the Holy Spirit. Why is it that the very first commandment is largely ignored?

Without answering that question we would like to emphatically declare: Revival comes when God's children obey the first commandment. It is that basic, and we have missed it for so long!

Moreover, loving God is something that is to be done. You do it. Jesus denounced the Pharisees for their meticulous tithing while they "passed over judgment and the love of God." Then he added concerning the tithing, "These ought ye to have done." But He did not stop there. He concluded, "And not leave the other undone."

What were they leaving undone? They were leaving the love of God undone. Probably 95 percent of the evangelicals today do not genuinely worship and adore God. They do not love Him. Mind you, they would say they do love God. But only superficially. Yet Jesus clearly implied that loving God is something one does. Do you do it?

The Rev. Charles G. Finney, beyond doubt the greatest revivalist in church history, was a Presbyterian minister whose powerful logic and fiery preaching brought hundreds of thousands to faith in Christ. We should not be surprised that he taught very strongly that love is something one does.

The command also begins very directly with the personal pronoun *you*. The Holy Spirit, I find, is that way. Direct and personal. This matter of loving God is for you, not someone else.

I will always recall a very important lesson the Lord taught me about personal pronouns. Just a year or so prior to graduation from Bible College, one of our teachers assigned a written speech. After much polishing, it was finally to be memorized and then delivered as part of a program in the churches in the main cities of Western Canada. The first drafts came back to me liberally splashed with red pencil. In one of the final drafts, my teacher asked for many corrections, and said very specifically, "You use the personal pronoun too much. Please eliminate the personal pronouns." Somewhat mischievously, I made all the corrections except the ones relating to the personal pronouns. I loved messages then with a forceful "you" in them—and still do.

My teacher, God bless her, forgot. I was allowed to memorize the message with all the personal pronouns intact. Then the message was delivered, along with the messages of other young people. God's presence and power was sensed everywhere. One service was especially memorable, and afterward my pastor, who had driven four hundred miles to attend, came up to me. "Neill," he said, with deep feeling, "always keep the 'you' in your preaching." I have never forgotten.

And like diamonds set on black velvet this text is studded with the personal pronoun "you." God expects *you* to love Him. It is something to be done and *you* do it.

And there is the word "all" repeated four times. *All* your heart, *all* your soul, *all* your mind, and *all* your strength. Such inclusiveness God requires. There is no room here for a 99 percent Christian commitment. And when we love God with *all,* that is revival!

Now let's talk about this matter of the heart.

There are two Greek words in the Scriptures which are commonly used for love. *Agapao* love refers to the kind of love that springs from the will, a deep love that is selfless and sacrificial. *Phileo* love is a more reserved, friendly kind of love. In fact, when Jesus was questioning Peter, He asked, "Do you love (*agapao*) me, Peter?" All Peter could summon from his heart so soon after his denial was, "Lord, thou knowest that I love (*phileo*) thee." Finally, the Saviour reduced the level of love. He asked Peter the third time if he loved him with *phileo* love. And Peter responded in kind.

Now what the Lord wants is the *agapao* love that springs from the will. When you love God with all your heart, it is not something that is necessarily emotional. The heart is the center of the will. You must decide to love God whether you feel like it or not. And then do it.

Dr. Mark Lee, a personal friend and a guest on two occasions at the Nakamun conferences, writes of an experience he and his wife shared.

"For a decade or so my wife and I lived, as we suppose other married couples do, thinking that we loved one another in appropriate marital fashion. It was the kind of affection that says, 'If you love me you will do this or that for me.' I now call this level of affection 'High School Love' because I had the experience several times in high school and observed my friends in a similar state. This is a selfish love which says, 'If you love me you will permit me to touch you, to do as I please with you.' It is something that does not really concern itself with the benefit of the object. Such a love uses rather than permits itself to be used. And that selfish spirit carried into our marriage."

Dr. Lee continues, "Our lives retained the usual adjustments and pressures found in marriage, and we felt that there was something lacking. Was married life, like all life's anticipations, reduced in the experience? No fulfillment is quite what we thought it would be. At length we struck upon the issue in our chats, spats, and devotional reading. Several persons were useful in illuminating the matter."

"Then we saw it. One day it rose like a shore on the horizon. It was like an island upon a vast sea on which we had been drifting. The love of *no motive* became clear and we beached our craft upon it. We will never leave that holy place, for it is the place of idyllic love. For us it is no longer, 'If you love me you will do this for me,' but 'I love you: hence, what may I do for you?' " [1]

I believe loving God is like that. You must love Him with all your heart. You must decide to do it and you must do it.

The text also says "with all your soul." Now we are all tripartite beings—body, soul and spirit. The body is world-conscious. The spirit is God-conscious. The soul is self-conscious.

And it is my conviction that there is a soulish area in our lives that must experience the cross and death to self before we may wholly love God with all our souls.

The saintly George M. Blackett, founder of the Canadian Bible College in Regina, said this, "There is an enemy within that is in league with the devil without." I could not agree more. The ego. The

---

[1] Mark W. Lee, *Our Children Are Our Best Friends,* Grand Rapids, Michigan: Zondervan Publishing House, 1970, pp. 65-66. Used with permission.

self. The big "I." The carnal nature. The old man is there. And it must die.

Strangely enough, the doctrine of death to self, which I had always considered at the least complicated and at the most very difficult to understand was the very doctrine that was running like a prairie fire across Western Canada. I had never realized that God's Word was so powerful nor that the Holy Spirit could illuminate thousands with new understanding in a matter of weeks. But it was happening.

An Evangelical Free Church pastor from central Alberta put it very clearly, "I do not believe we will ever understand the crucified life until the Holy Spirit gives us a revelation of the cross." God was giving the revelation. Revival is God's Holy Spirit probing the self life and enabling you to bring your selfish nature to the cross of Christ for a liberating death.

Dying to self can be very practical too. In the month of February I was invited by a number of churches to participate in the revival that was already underway in the Okanagan valley of British Columbia. It was while there that God gave me a wonderful experience in prayer. One day as I was praying, my wife and children came up before me. I felt that I had given them over to the Lord, but sensed that the Holy Spirit wanted more. So I determined to give these loved ones afresh to God. When I tried to do so the struggle I encountered was itself a lesson to me. I just could not give up my family completely into God's hands. But after perhaps ten minutes of agony in prayer, I said, "Lord, all the way, they are yours."

As the meetings in Penticton extended four

weeks I began to notice a freedom from lonesomeness. "Being an evangelist," I had always confided to my friends, "is wonderful, but there is a cross—leaving my family." I wondered if perhaps I was not lonesome because I was staying with my parents for that month in Penticton. Then on the phone my wife said, "Perhaps you are not lonesome because you have given us to God." That was it exactly.

And further experience confirmed it. My eight-week tour in the Philippines was practically without communication with home. The mail service to Mindanao is terribly slow. But there was no anguish. No loneliness.

The self-pity that for 10 years had made so many tours incredibly hard had been nailed to the cross. And I am convinced that death to self is a necessary antecedent to truly loving God with your soul. What about you?

The text goes on to say, "All thy mind." We are to love God with all our mind and all our strength. The mind. Here is the center of intelligence, of thought. The mind is the battleground for unseen forces. Satan's attack begins there. It is therefore important that our thoughts be centered on Christ, that we have a correct mental image of Him. Paul tells us that the carnal mind is enmity against God. We are to be transformed by the renewing of our mind; those who are spiritual are to have the mind of Christ. We are instructed to think about things that are honest, just, pure, lovely and of good report.

Our thoughts are a good gauge of where our true affections really lie. Those who love Christ with all their mind will find that unconsciously their thoughts revert to Him when they are not occupied with the necessary things of life. If we truly love Him nothing will be more delightful than to think about Him.

I am reminded also of the scripture, "Let this mind be in you, which was also in Christ Jesus, who, being in the form of God, thought it not robbery to be equal with God: but made himself of no reputation, and took upon him the form of a servant, and was made in the likeness of men: and being found in fashion as a man, he humbled himself, and became obedient unto death, even the death of the cross" (Philippians 2:5-8).

If you would love the Lord with all your mind you must humble yourself. It is impossible to be humble before God and proud and stiff-necked before people. In fact, God resists the proud. The devil does not need to resist them, God does.

On one occasion I was conducting meetings at Fort Nelson, mile 300 on the Alaska Highway. Strangely, I was aware of resistance but also knew that it was not the enemy. Later the Holy Spirit unmistakably showed me the cause. God Almighty was Himself committed to oppose me because of the pride in my heart.

Revival in Western Canada has been a continuing series of believers humbling themselves before one another. "Confess your sins one to another," say the Scriptures.

Scores of husbands and wives have asked one another's forgiveness. For example, a man who had formerly been a Christian worker but who had left the ministry was hard and bitter, serving God in a perfunctory kind of way. When revival came to Saskatoon, he began to be concerned.

Then the revolution of love came to his heart about four o'clock in the morning in what became known as "afterglows." When his wife confessed, "Please forgive me, I have not loved you as I ought to have," he was broken. His reserve was shattered by the humility of his wife and the genuine concern of several laymen.

Our observation in the Philippines was the same. In every case the launching pad for revival was, surprisingly enough, not prayer but humility and transparent honesty among Christians.

The revolution of love begins with humility. "If my people, which are called by my name, shall humble themselves, and pray, and seek my face, and turn from their wicked ways; then will I hear from heaven, and I will forgive their sin, and will heal their land" (II Chronicles 7:14).

And I do not hesitate to say it in print. Revival, the revolution of love, comes only to those who will love God enough to humble themselves before others.

One of my pastor friends put it this way, "Humbling is not something one does in private. Every time in the Scripture that a person humbles himself he does it publicly." It is impossible to be humble before God and stiff-necked before men and brethren.

Our text goes on to talk about loving God with "all your strength." The businessman goes early and late to be successful. The athlete trains vigorously and continuously. Should those who love God with all their strength have a lesser dedication? I think not.

A young pastor listening to these remarks was deeply impressed with this thought, "I do not love

God with all my strength," and so, in a public way before his people, he said, "Lord, I take this. I do love thee with all my heart, and all my soul, and all my mind and I will love thee with all my strength. I give all my strength to you." Then he stood up and addressed his people. "After hearing a message like this there is only one thing we can do. God has told us to love one another. Let us all go from one to the other expressing our love in the name of Jesus Christ."

One thing more—commands in the Word of God carry with them implicitly the power to obey. The Lord does not mock us when He asks us to love Him with all our hearts, souls, minds and strength. Moreover, obedience, in the case of this commandment, is completely revolutionary. It brings revival!

CHAPTER 8

To Your Neighbors

In the last chapter we discussed the vertical relationship—love for God. But there is a horizontal relationship as well.

In Mark 12:31 Jesus followed the first commandment with, "Thou shalt love thy neighbour as thyself. There is none other commandment greater than these."

In fact, as John made it clear, failure on the horizontal plane only indicates a lack of love for God in the first place. "If any man say, I love God, and hateth his brother, he is a liar; for he that loveth not his brother whom he hath seen, how can he love God whom he hath not seen?" (I John 4:20).

Again we have the personal pronoun "you." This commandment is not for someone else.

And we must insert here, just as loving God is something to be done, so loving your neighbor is something you do. There is a passage in I Thessalonians 4 which is amazingly clear, "But as touching brotherly love ye need not that I write unto you; for ye yourselves are taught of God to love one another. And indeed you *do* it..." (vss. 9-10).

It would be foolish to deny that love is an attitude, or that it must be shown in deeds. John also said, "Let us not love in word and tongue but in deed and truth." But still there are times when love must be done, must be expressed. Three of the most powerful words in all the world are found in the simple sentence, "I love you."

Implied here in Jesus' words is also a very basic truth about self-love. We have previously emphasized the necessity of dying to self, but this emphasis should not be misconstrued as a denunciation of all that is of self. There is a very real sense in which we cannot function efficiently or properly as Christians until we accept ourselves. Self-acceptance is as necessary as self-crucifixion. The Saviour made it clear that loving your neighbor was to have a comparative, a wholesome one— as you love yourself.

Now who is your neighbor?

First of course there is the man, the woman, the family that lives next to you. They are your neighbors and you are to love them. And sometimes they are unlovely.

One Christian friend shared this story. His neighbor needed help with house repairs. So he gave it. As compensation the neighbor told the believer that he could have a can of paint. Fine. But later the neighbor sent a bill for the can of paint. Perhaps the Christian should have paid but he did not. Then the neighbor took him to the small debts court. As a further aggravation, he threw his beer bottles on the believer's back lawn. Not quite so charitable and longsuffering as their father, the sons went out and threw the bottles back. Jesus said, "Love your neighbour." And chances are that he may be unlovely. But our duty is clear all the same.

And what about the people with whom you worship? Do you love your neighbor in church? So many professing Christians do not. Many churches are not famous for their soul-winning and missionary fervor—they are known instead for the guerrilla warfare carried on between members.

A Filipino woman was very descriptive, saying, "I used to go to church squinting, afraid I would see the other lady." They had quarreled over an insignificant item and the supposedly more mature squinter had refused to forgive. Yet, when revival came the "Christian squinter" went at 4:30 a.m. to be reconciled with her sister. Not all the "Christian squinters" are in the Philippines!

Loving your neighbor is as practical as loving your marriage partner. For the men the Scriptures specifically command, "Husbands, love your wives" (Ephesians 5:25). In a church where we ministered in General Santos City, on the island of Mindanao, a dentist was in attendance. I noticed the abundance of his tears and wondered about what God was speaking to him. (I found some difficulty in understanding his Filipino English.) But I soon learned what was happening. His wife put it this way, describing her husband's return from one of the early morning meetings, "For the first time after eight years of marriage, my husband woke me up with kisses and said, 'I love you.' I hope there are more revivals like this."

Another man in the same church put it this way, "After the service last night I wrote to my wife and told her, 'I love you.' And added the words, 'very much.' This I did for the first time."

Illustrations might be multiplied endlessly. Because one of the basic human needs is to be loved.

(The other is to love.) And love for your marriage partner is something that needs to be expressed verbally and shown through deeds and thoughtful behavior.

Loving your neighbor, for the wife, includes love for her husband. Tragically, for so many, all romance has long since skipped out of the marriage, and revival is, among other things, a rekindling of romantic love in the home.

A fine Christian woman from Alberta listened thoughtfully to these concepts. Her husband is an alcoholic and her love for him had ebbed away. But she went home to say to her husband, "I love you." He was of course shocked, but in a lovely kind of way. Her testimony later was clear and vibrant, "God has renewed my love for my husband; it had not been extinguished but it had been covered by so many things."

In the Philippines, we discovered that the women respond much as do their Canadian counterparts. After one service a matronly woman, well-to-do, efficient and prosperous in business, told her husband that she loved him. He was so shocked he sat bolt upright in bed.

Admittedly the expression of love is not a problem to everyone, but for many it is pulling the key log out of the logjam. A flood of pent-up emotion is likely to follow. And ultimately completely new life-patterns are formed.

"Love is the medicine for the sickness of the world,"[1] said the compassionate physician, Karl Menninger, and we might properly add, "Love

---

[1] Bruce Larson, *Dare to Live Now*, Grand Rapids, Michigan: Zondervan Publishing House, 1965, p. 37. Used with permission.

is the medicine for the sickness of the church and home."

Loving your neighbor also involves your children. Incredibly enough, there are many "Christian" homes where one or several or even all of the little ones are unloved.

Some parents have favorites. They lavish their love upon one child to the neglect of the others. Judge Brillante was like that. He and his gracious wife have seven children. The Filipino judge is also a new believer and very anxious to walk carefully with God. When revival exploded in their church, the judge was one of the first to respond. The Holy Spirit had pointed out that one of his daughters was his favorite while at the same time he lacked love for his little boy. There was no recourse but to go to the boy and beg forgiveness. With tears the man of God did just that. "Bobo," he said, "please forgive me for not loving you."

Mrs. Brillante had a similar issue to meet. She lacked love for the daughter who just happened to be her husband's favorite! And she lavished her love upon Bobo.

The failure to properly love one's own children is not just something the Holy Spirit talks about to others. My wife and I have had to face the very same issue in our own heart. But thank God, revolutionary changes came when this root problem was finally recognized, faced, and dealt with by our Lord.

Love for neighbors also includes parents. For young people the acid test of love is obedience—obedience to parents. And in the adolescent years especially, obedience to parents is hard. But there is no alternative. Obedience is love's response.

Also, evangelistic fervor is a true reflection of love for one's neighbor. If you believe your neighbor is eternally lost, you will certainly do something to reach him. A love for God which evades or avoids evangelistic responsibility is a spurious love. The church groups which are the most evangelistic are the ones who genuinely show their love for their neighbors.

Love your neighbors. It is the true revolution, the revolution of love.

CHAPTER 9
And Your Enemies Too

It is one thing to properly respect and love yourself, to love God wholly and to love your neighbor. It is yet another to love one another *as* Christ loved His disciples. And probably these commands are impossible without divine motivation and help.

But there is an impossible of the impossibles. Jesus said, "Love your enemies! Pray for those who persecute you! In that way you will be acting as true sons of your Father in heaven" (Matthew 5:44-45, Living Bible).

In some parts of the world the impossible command may not seem so applicable, but in Ulster, for example, it means Catholics must love Protestants and Protestants must love Catholics.

In the Middle East it means Arabs must love Jews and Jews must love Arabs. In some parts of the United States it means whites must love blacks and blacks must love whites. In other countries it means Moslems must love Christians and Christians must love Moslems. That such a list could be endless is itself a sorrowful reflection upon humanity.

But some may question here. These people about whom you speak are not deeply committed Christian believers.

And that is true. But there are "Christian enemies," if you know what I mean—people in the rank and file and sometimes in the leadership of our evangelical churches who know only too well how to hate. And if the revolution of love will do anything, it will shatter these enmities and heal these hatreds.

Like that of the anguished wife and mother who confessed to practicing with a shotgun with a view to murder because her husband was unfaithful to her.

Like that of the new and sincere convert who in a moment of passion said of her believing sister, "I hate her."

Like that of Evangeline whose flashing black eyes narrowed to slits as she thought about the young people in the choir. "I hate them," she hissed.

Like that of the teen-age boy whose thoughts focused on his profligate father and the bitter words spilled out. "I hate him!"

Like that of the young man struggling in prayer who could not believe until the confession of his bondage exploded from his lips. "I hate my pastor!"

But enmity and hatred can be conquered.

Our Lord's death on the cross is the prime example. He had been mutilated, His back shredded with the Roman lash, His hands and feet torn by the ragged Roman spikes. He was dying in the hands of hatred. Still, His prayer was victorious and compassionate, "Father, forgive them, for they know not what they do."

Fox's Book of Martyrs is filled with the accounts of those who, like the Saviour, died with forgiveness on their lips.

Perhaps the more difficult thing is to love and forgive those who taunt but never touch, those who hate but never hit.

Love your enemies. Pray for your persecutors. Such actions irrevocably pit themselves against the grain of human nature, the natural order.

And spiritual revolution upsets the established order. With so many doing the natural thing, Christ calls and commands us to do the supernatural. Then He gives us the strength to love and to do.

CHAPTER 10
Observable Love

"Selfishness," said A. B. Simpson, "is in defiance of the law of Christ . . . He gave to His disciples a law of love even higher than that of the Old Testament. It is no longer 'Thou shalt love thy neighbour as thyself,' but it is 'Love one another as I have loved you.' " [1]

Yes, the new commandment is clear enough. "Little children, yet a little while I am with you. Ye shall seek me: and as I said unto the Jews, Whither I go, ye cannot come; so now I say to you, A new commandment I give unto you, That ye love one another; as I have loved you, that ye also love one another. By this shall all men know that ye are my disciples, if ye have love one to another" (John 13:33-34).

Jesus is saying something very important, exceedingly so. It is important because He said it. It is important because John emphasized it. And it is important because of the timing.

Three things happen earlier in the 13th chapter of John.

First there is the unusual expression of love in John's reporting. Kenneth N. Taylor paraphrases

---

[1] A. B. Simpson, "Meditations in the Word," *Alliance Witness*, December 20, 1972, p. 22.

the opening words this way, "And how he loved his disciples!" (John 13:1, Living Bible).

Secondly, in a striking act of demonstrated humility and love, Jesus washes the feet of His disciples. Ordinarily, it would have been the duty of a slave to wash the feet of guests who had come in off the dusty streets. But Jesus insisted on doing it.

Peter's reaction always fascinates me. He wanted no part of the footwashing. "No, you shall never wash my feet!" But when Jesus explained that to refuse meant to have no part with Him, Peter changed his tune. "Lord," he said, "I'll have a bath!" Such is the force of the original language.

It was in this context that Jesus gave His new commandment, "Love one another as I have loved you."

Following the act of footwashing, there was the feast of the Passover. It was there that John leaned upon Jesus' breast—as someone has said—just because he wanted to. Such was his love for the Master. It was also there that Satan entered into Judas bodily. It was there that Jesus said to him, "That thou doest, do quickly."

Certainly it was a tense moment for Judas, and perhaps for our Lord. Full of high drama.

Then the betrayer went out, bent on quisling treachery. But he did not go unloved, nor with his feet unwashed.

It was in this context that Jesus delivered His new commandment. As He was about to give it, He again told His disciples of His departure. "Moreover," He explained, "where I am going you'll not be able to follow." Surely nothing could have been clearer.

"So now I say unto you." "So I am giving a new commandment to you," one translator puts it.

Incredible. But clear. The love springing from obedience to this new commandment Jesus was about to give was intended to *replace His physical presence.*

Love. The substitute for His physical presence. (Later, He explained that the Comforter was coming, Who would guide into all truth. The two currents of truth seem to flow together here, for the fruit of the Spirit is love. And, as another commentator has pointed out, joy, peace, longsuffering, gentleness, goodness, faith, meekness and temperance all form golden sections of the same orange—love.)

"By this shall all men know." The world would be instantly able to identify Christians—by their love. I like Schaeffer's phrase, "observable love." [2] The young people have been singing for several years, "They'll know we are Christians by our love."

The world will know us by our love. And how does anyone know anything? Through the senses, of course.

Though some might argue that love can be smelled and tasted, we think not. But love can be *heard.* In January of 1972 I made one of many missionary journeys I have taken into Cree Indian territory. At a place called Peerless Lake, one hundred and fifty miles northeast of High Prairie, Alberta, I shared for two days with the lovely Indian believers. For the whole two days I talked about

---

[2] Francis A. Schaeffer, *The Church at the End of the 20th Century,* Downers Grove, Illinois: Inter-Varsity Press, 1970, p. 139.

love. Their black eyes glistened and their hearts responded.

Because most of their conversation was in Cree I could not know what was happening. But something surely was. "Sakahaytin" was the word. They were going from one to another saying, "Sakahaytin"—I love you. They seemed even more responsive to the message of love than their white brothers and sisters in the outside world. And their expression of love was completely spontaneous. Six months later I saw some of them again. They greeted me as before, "Sakahaytin."

Love among Christians is to be observable. It needs to be *heard*—with words like "Sakahaytin."

The world also has the right to *see* it among us. But often they do not. If I dare to be honest with you, I have moved among evangelicals nearly all my life—and have seen very little love.

But thank God, I *have* seen it. As we have already mentioned in these pages, the Rev. Carmelo Terranova, Argentine evangelist and Bible teacher, was with us in the 1971 Nakamun convention.

As sometimes happens in a camp, a number of the tents and cabins were entered covertly. Around two hundred dollars had been taken and everyone was rather upset. The two boys who had done it were caught and brought fearfully to their parents. One of my preacher friends said to me, "I think we ought to go and talk straight and hard to those boys." We set out for their tent trailer with those intentions.

What a mistake we made! We took with us the man of love, Mr. Terranova. When we entered the tent trailer everyone was very uneasy. Only one of the boys was present.

Then Mr. Terranova spoke to me in Spanish.

"Tell the boy to come and sit beside me." I did so. "Tell him to look up." So I asked the boy to look up; which he did. Then our dear brother, who had come eight thousand miles to show us how to love, bent over and kissed the wayward boy. With a Spanish accent he said in English, "I love you." The boy had been hard, but now there were tears in his eyes. We all were in tears. Somehow there was nothing more to say.

I stumbled out of the tent trailer into the sunlight, nearly blinded with tears. And only one thought pulsed back and forth through my mind. "I have *seen* First Corinthians thirteen. I have *seen* First Corinthians thirteen."

Love is to be *heard, seen,* and *felt* if the world is going to know we are Christians by our love.

Barely three days after twenty-three people had been massacred in the Mindanao town of Ipil, we passed through it. Everyone was tense. People were fleeing if they were able. Anywhere—just to get away. And I *felt* the hatred and fear there. Everyone did.

Now if we can feel hate and fear, how much more ought the world to be able to feel the love that Christ intended to be the mark of the Christian atmosphere?

In talking about the roots of the Canadian revival in chapter three, I mentioned the outpouring of love at Nakamun. Mr. Terranova was preaching. Finally he said to the people, "Tell your brother beside you that you love him." He persisted until the people began to obey him. And though it seems cold and mechanical in print, in the atmosphere of that hour it was vibrant and alive, very much in the Spirit.

Suddenly something broke. Perhaps it was our

Anglo-Saxon reserve giving way before the unction of the Holy Spirit and Latin persuasiveness. Though words are inadequate, there was an explosion of love. It seemed as if the camp grounds were covered with love. And who is to say they were not? Hundreds of witnesses would agree; you could "feel" it. And when revival came later to Saskatoon, we had no trouble understanding our brethren when they said, "We are wading knee-deep in love."

Now I am proposing here that the world has a right to "hear" and "see" and "feel" Christ's love among us.

And when they become aware of the love among us, they will come easily to the feet of Jesus.

Something certainly happened to Simon Peter. To begin with, he was the reluctant disciple who could offer only friendly *phileo* love to His Saviour. But later in his writings the Holy Spirit obviously flows through a different man. "See that ye love one another with a pure heart fervently." "Have fervent love among yourselves, for love shall cover the multitude of sins."

CHAPTER 11
That Bad Dog

There are three obstacles to the revolution of love in our hearts, and possibly the worst one of all is the bad dog!

But let me explain. Revival is not for the world, though certainly it profoundly affects the world. It is new life for the church. And there are obstacles to personal revival. We all know, for example, that Satan is an enemy. Does not the Word say, "Be sober, be vigilant, because your adversary, the devil, like a roaring lion walketh about, seeking whom he may devour"? (I Peter 5:9).

And what must we do with the devil? Certainly he must be refused. The ground we have given him, knowingly or unknowingly, we need to retrieve and put in the hand of the Lord Jesus Christ. And it is often best to take back that ground audibly in a deliberate act of the will. It is a spiritual law that God makes real to you what you *say* in faith.

There are oppressive attacks of the enemy as well. That is when he needs to be resisted, and indeed, he will flee from us.

And if one encounters demon possession, as is more and more frequently the case in these days, then the promise is clear: "These signs shall follow them that believe: In my name they shall cast out devils" (Mark 16:17). When one is positive that the case is actually demonic possession repetitious, commanding is sometimes necessary to dislodge the enemy. In one case Jesus kept saying to the enemy, "Come out of the man, you unclean spirit." (See Mark 5:8 in the Amplified New Testament.)

Also, to avoid complications and transferences, workers should be careful to send the conquered spirits to the abyss. In the case of the Legion, the swine ran down a steep place into the deep (abyss in the original).

But Satan is not the only enemy of revival. There is sin. Sin is the transgression of the law. It is the failure to do good. And all of us are guilty.

And the remedy? First of all, there is the confession of that sin to God. The word confess means to "say the same thing." If we are confessing our habit of lying to God, we certainly do not say, "Oh God, forgive me for being naughty." Instead we must say, "Oh God, I am a liar, please forgive me."

Further, we have not committed the sins in packages. They have been committed one by one, and as much as is possible, we ought to confess them one by one to God. "If we confess our sins, he is faithful and just to forgive us our sins, and to cleanse us from all unrighteousness" (I John 1:9).

There are times when confession to God is not enough. Sometimes we must confess our sins one to another. "Confess your sins one to another, and pray one for another, that ye may be healed" (James 5:16).

In the event that some may wish to hide behind

the word "fault," which appears in the King James Version, we hasten to add that the original word is "sin."

Confessing one's sins to another brother is not a papal practice. It is instead an act of humility which often kindles the spark of revival. Obviously if I have stolen ten dollars it is not enough to confess that sin to God, who will certainly forgive. I must also return the money in repentance to the one from whom I have stolen. Restitution when possible is yoked with repentance and confession.

A Filipino businessman was angry with his pastor. He had run for city council and lost by less than 500 votes; he blamed his pastor for not supporting him wholeheartedly. Eventually the relationship became so cool that he left the church in which he had come to know the Lord.

He found himself unhappy in his new house of worship and eventually drifted back to his old pastor. But the association was tense. Then at a convention at which they both were delegates they found themselves at an altar of reconciliation. They tearfully forgave one another and were reconciled. Not surprisingly, revival broke out in their church and God used them in other parts of their country as well to spark revival and spread the flame. Such is the power of confession.

But there is a more deceitful enemy than either Satan or sin. It is the ogre "self." All too often he is unrecognized and for that reason all the more deadly. It is the old man. The flesh. The carnal nature. There are many names for the big "I."

There is a story which is appropriate. Whether or not it is true does not really matter. An Eskimo, so we are told, was talking to a missionary and he confided, "I have two dogs inside me." The missionary was startled. "What are they like?" "Well," replied the Eskimo, "one is bad and one is good." "But what do they do?" "They fight." "And which one wins?" The Eskimo was quiet for a moment and then he answered very honestly, "Sometimes the bad dog wins; and sometimes the good one. It all depends on which one I say 'sic 'em' to."

The flesh is the bad dog.

The Bible teaching is clear. "Our old man is crucified with him, that the body of sin might be destroyed, that henceforth we should not serve sin" (Romans 6:6). The bad dog is already crucified.

Speaking of himself, Paul expressed it another way. "I am crucified with Christ; nevertheless I live, yet not I, but Christ liveth in me; and the life which I now live in the flesh I live by the faith of the Son of God, who loved me, and gave himself for me" (Galatians 2:20).

Any way you look at it, the bad dog has been dealt with by the cross. The bad dog in us was nailed to the back side of the cross when Jesus died.

But even though this is an indisputable theological fact, we continue to fight a losing battle to this enemy within. Every imaginable form of selfishness, pride, self-righteousness, sensitiveness, immorality, resentment, bitterness and hatred is present in the lives of professing Christians. Far from being revived we wallow in defeat.

And what is the answer? Petting the pooch and saying "Nice doggie" will hardly do. Tying him up will not help. He always breaks his leash at the most inappropriate times.

No, the dog must die—as adorable as he may sometimes seem. "Likewise reckon ye also yourselves to be dead indeed unto sin, but alive unto God through Jesus Christ our Lord" (Romans 6:11).

But how can it be done? A missionary friend in Guatemala once shared with me a priceless gem of spiritual wisdom. He said, "The Holy Spirit has come into the world to make real all that Jesus has purchased for us on the cross."

In that instant I understood more clearly than ever before. The preaching of the cross is the power of God for *saved* people (I Cor. 1:18). Thank God.

And exactly how is the bad dog put to the death? "If ye through the Spirit do mortify [make dead] the deeds of the body, ye shall live" (Romans 8:13).

By the Spirit. Of course.

And when I begin to deliberately and audibly say, "By the Holy Spirit I now crucify," naming the particular manifestation of self, the Christ-life becomes a reality.

Some try to cast out or confess self but it cannot be done. When one dear missionary was asking God to forgive her selfishness the Holy Spirit stopped her. He said, "Stop praying like that. Self cannot be forgiven; it must die."

And we might add, so resilient is this bad dog that he has to be reckoned dead every moment of every day.

Sometimes we misapply a remedy because we do not see the problem clearly. To the Africans we explained it this way. There once was a man who had a motor scooter that wouldn't start and a donkey that wouldn't work. So he purchased some gasoline and picked up a huge stick. Going over to the donkey, he tipped its head back and poured the gasoline down its throat. Then he seized the stick and gave the motor bike a good pounding. His remedies were right but his applications were wrong.

Sin must be confessed; Satan must be resisted, renounced and sometimes cast out; and self must die. To try to cast out self, for example, or crucify sin, is to misapply the divine remedy.

And as we are emphasizing especially here, the bad dog must die.

Deliver him over today.

Then pray for the release of God's purity and love. It will be a spiritual explosion. The revolution of love. In a word, revival.

CHAPTER 12

The Chariot Has Brakes

"One of the most important things in the Christian life," I was once told, "is to keep balanced." And nowhere is this more important than in the handling of the theme of love.

Charles G. Finney wrote at length about the attributes of love. He observed that love is voluntary, compassionate, merciful, truthful, meek, longsuffering, stable and kind. But he also noted that love is impartial, just and even severe.

"They greatly err," Finney said, "who suppose that benevolence is all softness under all circumstances. Severity is not cruelty but is love manifesting strictness, rigor, and purity when occasion demands. Love is universal good-will, or willing the highest good of being in general. When therefore anyone or any number so conduct themselves as to interfere with and endanger the public good, severity is just as natural and as necessary to benevolence as kindness and forbearance under other circumstances." [1]

In our discussion of love for God and man we must make clear that love is more than the trite

---

[1] Charles G. Finney, *Attributes of Love*, Minneapolis, Minnesota: Bethany Fellowship, Inc., 1963, p. 93.

mouthing of the newest evangelical cliché, "I love you."

Agape love for God and men springs from the will. It is inseparable from the will. Since there are various kinds of love, it is possible for *agape* (divine) love to finally be reduced to *phileo* (friendly) love or even *eros* (sensual) love. Conceivably those who meet God in revival love could finally succumb to its distortion, immorality.

True love is inseparable from the will. And in fact, emotion will invariably follow the will. But it should not lead it.

A familiar story illustrates this well. A man was walking down a wilderness path very much occupied with his own thoughts. Suddenly he looked up to discover a large bear looming over him. He did what any sensible man would do. He ran like crazy. Once in his cabin with the door slammed shut, he slumped into a chair. Paralyzed with fear.

Now what if emotion had been first? But it was not. First there was the exercise of the will. He ran. It was only later that the emotion flooded in.

Again, love is inseparable from deeds. We have established in these pages, we hope effectively, that love is something to be seen, heard and expressed. It is certainly something you do. And say.

But love is more than speech. "Let us stop saying we love people," Kenneth Taylor paraphrases; "let us really love them and show it by our actions" (I John 3:16, Living Bible). Deeds, then, demonstrate love.

God's *agape* love is also irrevocably linked with

true Christian faith. "Beloved, let us love one another: for love is of God; and everyone that loveth is born of God, and knoweth God" (I John 4:7).

On the negative side, John put it this way, "Whosoever hateth his brother is a murderer; and ye know that no murderer hath eternal life abiding in him" (I John 3:15). "By this shall all men know that ye are my disciples, if ye have love one to another" (John 13:35).

Nor can God's love be separated from the fulness of the Holy Spirit. "Be not drunk with wine, wherein is excess, but be filled with the Spirit" (Ephesians 5:18) is a plain scriptural command. And the fruit of the Spirit is love. Any experience, no matter how biblical it may seem to be, which does not shed abroad the love of God in our hearts cannot ever be construed to be the fulness of the Holy Spirit.

"God so loved . . . that he gave" (John 3:16), reflects another vital principle. God's love is a giving love. Mark Lee calls it the "no motive" love. A love which demands nothing in return. And any love which does not give, both materially and spiritually, must not in any circumstances be called God's love.

God's love, we have already suggested, is not "namby pamby." Rather it has a spine of steel. To be loving does not at all require that a man be naive and silly-soft.

Often I have had personal difficulty here—mistaking softheartedness for true love. Love can be and must sometimes be stern. Chastening, for example, is an expression of love. "Whom the Lord loveth, he chasteneth" (Hebrews 12:6).

Finally, and most importantly, love is inseparable from obedience. "By this we know that we love the children of God, when we love God, and keep his commandments. For this is the love of God, that we keep his commandments" (I John 5:2, 3).

A love for God which will not allow us to humble ourselves, deny self, and continually acknowledge the Lordship of Jesus Christ must be a spurious love.

The writings of St. Paul beautifully reflect the balance we wish to portray. "Make love your aim, and earnestly desire the spiritual gifts" (I Corinthians 14:1). "And this I pray, that your love may abound yet more and more in knowledge and in all judgment" (Philippians 1:9).

CHAPTER 13

The Logic of Love

In December of 1971, *Communicate*, our own periodical, published my wife's testimony which she first titled, "The Mark of a Christian." Later, for the sake of clarification, another title was added, "How I Learned to Love."

One thing became immediately clear. Though our circulation at that time was small, not much more than 4,000 copies, the letter response from the article was unusual.

As an introduction to the testimony, I include some of those letters here.

> "Your article on the 'Mark of a Christian' was just wonderful. We wanted to keep it so my husband made a photo copy of it. Now I see that you offer them in tract form and I would like three dozen of them."
>
> P.B.

> "We had a Know Your Bible Fellowship last night and the theme was love and the article on the 'Mark of a Christian' was read ... I told my husband last night that I loved him for the first time in ages and I want to continue loving the Lord first and loving others. I wonder if by chance there would be an extra copy that I could have so that I could read and reread and continually have it before me ..."
>
> G.A.

"I just have to tell you what God has done for me. I'm so filled with praise to Him that I just can't love Him enough. He has become so real to me, and my only desire is to love Him with all my heart and soul and mind."

G.

"Really enjoyed your article in *Communicate* on love. Portions of it were read as a devotional at our last ladies' meeting and I know it spoke to others as it did to me."

J.S.

"I am delighted to hear from your recent paper *Communicate*, March 1972, that the article 'The Mark of a Christian' is available in tract form. The Holy Spirit made this article very precious to me and I have used it and loaned it till it is almost threadbare. I know I will be able to extend its ministry largely with tracts."

H.M.D.

Now the rest of this chapter is my wife's testimony, "How I learned to Love."

What is the mark of a Christian?

Before Christ died, He wanted to prepare the disciples for His death and what was to follow. He wanted them to realize what the distinguishing feature or mark of every Christian would be. John 13:34-35 tells us. "A new commandment I give unto you, That ye love one another; as I have loved you, that ye also love one another. *By this shall all men know that ye are my disciples, if ye have love one to another.*" Love was to be the distinguishing mark of a Christian.

Now why did God make love the mark of a

Christian? Why did not God say, "By this shall all men know that ye are my disciples if ye live holy lives? If ye are generous and give to the poor? If ye wear sombre, drab clothing? If ye wear a cross around your neck or a certain lapel pin? If ye greet each other with the peace sign?" Why did Christ specifically say that the distinguishing feature of a Christian was to be love?

In the beginning God faced two possibilities. One was to make men robots, programmed to do, say, and think as He dictated. But God wanted obedience, not out of necessity, but out of love. So He created humans as free moral agents, implying that all men have three characteristics: emotions, intelligence and will. Any one of these can control others. The intelligence can control the emotions, the emotions can control the intelligence, and of course the will can control either of these. However, the emotions or the intelligence cannot control the will without its agreement. The will always has the power to resist the force of either the intelligence or the emotions. It is not compelled to obey them. The entire tone of our lives is determined by whichever factor we allow to be in control.

God gave Adam and Eve the opportunity to exercise their power of choice by telling them that they could eat of every fruit in the garden except of the fruit of the tree in the midst of the garden. Eve had two alternatives—to obey God or to disobey Him.

She chose to disobey. Why did Eve disobey God? Essentially, she disobeyed because she wanted her own way instead of His. Wanting our own way is called selfishness. In other words, selfishness is obedience to what we feel like doing, to what our emotions tell us to do. It is the obedience of the will to the emotions. The selfish person does what he feels like doing, thinking only of the benefits of the action to himself and not to others.

Disobedience to God is selfishness because we are choosing our own way and not God's. *Selfishness is the obedience of the will to the emotions.*

The other alternative which presented itself to Eve was to obey God. If to disobey God is selfishness, then to obey God is love. For love is the opposite of selfishness. Love is giving all of one's self for the highest good of another or others.

We said that free moral agents have three attributes: intelligence, emotions and will, and that selfishness is the obedience of the will to the emotions. What then is love? *Love is the obedience of the will to the intelligence.* Love is obedience to what we know to be right and true.

What is it that we know? We know the facts of history and we know what the Bible says. The Bible says (and it is also a fact of history) that God's Son came to this earth as a baby. He was the Son of God, but also the Son of man, for He was born of a woman, a virgin. We know that He lived a sinless life, and after a brief ministry, was taken away and crucified. Why did He thus die? the Bible says, "For God so loved the world, that he gave his only begotten Son, that whosoever believeth in him should not perish but have everlasting life."

That was why He died—to reconcile to God those that He had made in the first place for fellowship with Him and who had, through selfishness, through wanting their own way, gone away from Him and turned their back on His way to follow their own way. These are scriptural facts and our intelligence is aware of them.

Now the Bible also tells us that if we accept Christ's way, His salvation, then we are new creatures in Christ Jesus, all things are become new. Then it is no longer our way, it is God's way. It is no longer what we desire, it is what God desires. That is what repentance means—turning from our own way to walk in the way of the Lord. Now if doing our own will and going our own way is selfishness, doing God's will and going His way is love!

Love is the obedience of the will to the intelligence. The love that God requires then is not the love or affection of the emotions; not the love that feels like loving. He requires the love of the will, that loves because it should love and because it chooses to love. Our will must rule, not our emotions.

The Bible tells us that God is love. This one word "love" describes the totality of God. We said earlier that to love means to desire the highest good of someone else and to give of one's self completely for the other person. This is God!

He desires our highest good, not His own, else He would not have robbed His only Son of all the glories of heaven and sent Him down to this sin-polluted earth to suffer unspeakable indignities and to die for mankind. Neither would Jesus Christ, the Son, have humbled Himself, submitting His will to the will of His Father. He was not forced to do it, for He is God. But God the Father knew that that was the only way that mankind could be brought back into fellowship with Him. God loved us enough to make that sacrifice—His only Son. And God loves us enough that still these many years later, the offer of pardon is open for all who will accept it. That is love. God's love.

"We love Him because He first loved us." We give our best to Him because He first gave His best for us.

Love encompasses all other virtues. A. B. Simpson says that the fruit of the Spirit is love—joy, peace, longsuffering, gentleness, goodness, faith, meekness and temperance. These virtues are all only attributes of love. The fruit of the Spirit is love, period.

Paul goes on to say that against love there is no law. "Now we are delivered from the law," says the scripture. Christ came to do that. He wants our obedience, not because the law demands it, but because we choose, motivated by love, to obey Him.

These then are the two alternatives—selfishness or love. Disobedience to God, or obedience to God.

You say, "How can I love God?" The answer is simple—will to love Him, choose to love Him. It doesn't matter what our emotions tell us, what we feel like doing. No, it is what we will to do, what our goal is, what we are setting out to do. If we choose to disobey God, that is selfishness. If we choose to obey God, that is love.

Only the Christian can truly love because to love means to obey God joyfully and unquestioningly. Love is the mark of the Christian.

Now may I share with you how I learned to love? I had never really learned to love. Oh yes, I had some of that kind of love that comes from the emotions. But I had never truly learned to love.

For a long time I didn't realize it. My husband would ask me, "Why don't you tell me that you love me?" Do you know why I didn't tell him more often that I loved him? Because I didn't want it to be a lie. I didn't always feel that I loved him. Once in a while when I "felt loving" I would tell him, but those times could be counted up in a hurry. He'd say, "Do you love me?" And I'd say, "Of course," or "Don't ask such silly questions," or "What do you think?" as if to say that that was a stupid question to ask. After all, aren't wives supposed to love their husbands?

Each time that I would say, "Of course," in response to his question, something inside me would say, "Do you really? Do you really know what it means to love at all, or what loving is all about?"

This all began to bother me. And it bothered me so much that finally I admitted to the Lord that maybe there was something wrong with me, and maybe I did need to learn to love.

I told the Lord that day, "When I see someone who knows how to love, not in this way that I think I love, but in the right way, in Your way, then I will talk with him." Now I had never confided in anyone in all my life, not in my parents nor my husband, nor in any minister. So to promise the Lord that I would seek counsel was quite a step in itself.

Then this past summer (1971) the Argentine evangelist, Carmelo Terranova, came to our home and preached in our church. It was evident that he was a man who knew how to love, a man that loved in a way that few people I had ever met knew how to love. The Lord worked in my heart and I wept through much of the message. I felt that he would understand my need. We would be meeting several days hence at Nakamun Family Camp, so I purposed then in my heart to talk to him as I had promised the Lord sometime before.

The Lord used the first few messages at camp to speak directly to me. I couldn't help but weep through them. And then one day, I arranged to have an interview with Mr. Terranova. Of course he asked what I wanted. And I said, "Well, I suppose to put it briefly, I want to learn to love." There, it was out!

We talked for a while and his counsel to me was very simple. "You must start by saying, 'I love you.' This is where you have the difficulty and this is where you must begin."

Now I felt like arguing with him. Wasn't it a lie to say, "I love you," when you didn't really feel like it? "No," he said, "don't worry about that. Just start saying it and the feeling will come." So I reasoned (there's the intelligence), I've come to him for counsel because I felt he had the answer for me. Am I going to argue or am I going to take his advice?

I decided that I had better take his advice. I started first by saying to the Lord, "I love you, Lord." Now that was hard enough. But to say it to my husband, that was something else! At first I kind of said it in passing. He nearly fainted!

And then to the children. I used to say, "Mommy loves you." That was a nice convenient "third person" way of getting around it. Now I said "I love you, Tim; I love you, Donna; I love you, Jeff." Oh, it was hard, very hard. But surprise of surprises, the feeling started to come. And it really came! I could lift my hands to the Lord and say from the depths of my heart, "Lord, I love you, I love you, Lord." And I could say to my husband and to the children and to other Christians, "I love you," and really mean it!

What freedom this all brought! Those walls inside me began to fall. You see, when we truly love and are giving ourselves for the good of others, we leave ourselves open to hurt and we make ourselves vulnerable. I didn't want to be vulnerable, so I had built up walls around my heart to protect myself. But by saying, "I love you," and by shedding tears, something else which I had always hated to do, especially in front of people, the walls began to fall. I could feel it inside—a crack here, a piece falling there, and finally one wall after another tumbling down. Praise the Lord for this wonderful freedom!

Love is supreme. If we love God we will obey Him. If we love Him we will want to be with Him, and we will do all within our power to spend as much time as possible with Him. I can't begin to tell here of the wonderful times I have with the Lord each day reading His love letter to me and talking with Him.

If we love God, it follows too that we will love others. It is a natural sequence. And if we love others, then all our relationships with our brothers and sisters in Christ will be conducted accordingly.

If we love God, we will love the lost. God's love will motivate us to share Christ with them.

To love God is to obey Him and to obey Him is to love Him.

We are not constrained by duty, but by love. Our devotions are not a duty, but a joy. Witnessing is not a duty, but a joy. We are not doing it because we are forced to, but because we love.

The basis is love. Do you love Him? Do you will to love Him, to obey Him, or do you will to gratify self, to disobey Him? Let us will to love the Lord. How do we do it? Simply by choosing to do it.

Lord, I will, I choose to love you. Lord, I love you.

Say it and mean it, whether you feel like it or not—God will do the rest!

—Marilynne E. Foster

CHAPTER 14
The Fulness of Love

If the fruit of the Spirit is love and, as Paul explains, "the love of God is shed abroad in our hearts by the Holy Ghost" (Romans 5:8), then the fulness of the Holy Spirit is absolutely vital to any teaching on love. After all, God Himself is love.

In past years I have always winced a bit when I have heard some of the older saints praying "Lord, fill us with thy love." No more. Terminology is not that important. But reality is. And the revolution of love has brought reality to thousands of Christians.

There are obvious dangers in setting out one's points: one, two, three. Usually, the Holy Spirit is much more imaginative and responsive than our sterile logic would dictate.

Nevertheless, for clarity's sake, if nothing else, here is how I believe you can be filled with God's love and the Holy Spirit.

1. You must be saved. Saved is a biblical word. "Believe on the Lord Jesus Christ and thou shalt be saved, and thy house" (Acts 16:31), is still very good Bible teaching.

The Campus Crusade for Christ movement has made it increasingly clear to thousands of evangelicals who wish to share their faith, that God has a wonderful plan for all. But men, all of them, have sinned and spoiled God's plan. Fortunately, God has supplied a remedy through Christ's sacrificial death on the cross. And the Crusade people properly conclude, salvation must be individually and personally received. "As many as received him, to them gave he power to become the sons of God" (John 1:12).

For those of you who are perhaps not even religious but have been reading this book, searching for the revolution of love, I have something very important to say to you.

You must be saved. You must know Christ personally. And when you have found Him you will know it. "The Spirit himself bears witness with our spirit, that we are the children of God" (Romans 8:16).

The gate that leads to the revolution of love is spiritual conversion. It is the only gate and there is no other approach to God but through His Son Jesus Christ. "There is one mediator between God and man, the man Christ Jesus" (1 Timothy 2:5).

2. You must have a right motive. Amazingly enough, thousands of Christian believers seek God with wrong motives.

"We must decide," said one man of God, "whether the Holy Spirit is a power that we are to take hold of and use, or whether the Holy Spirit is a personal being Who is to take hold of and use us."

3. You must be obedient. Acts 5:32 speaks of "the Holy Ghost, whom God hath given to them that obey him." Obedience is what a rebellious and unregenerate heart resents and resists. On

the other side, obedience is the Christian's key to power and blessing. Included in obedience is consecration, surrender, yieldedness, confession and restitution. The all-inclusive word *obedience* allows for no resistance, resentment or rebellion. It calls instead for a military and instant response to God. This obedience in every area of life is a condition for the fulness of love.

There is no better rule for the hungry heart than, "Whatsoever he saith unto you, do it" (John 2:5).

4. You must dethrone self. Earlier in this book we have made clear that the self-life is an obstacle to the fulness of the Spirit and the revolution of love. Death to self is the door to life in the Spirit. "For the law of the Spirit of life in Christ Jesus hath made me free from the law of sin and death" (Romans 8:2).

5. You must be spiritually hungry. "They that hunger and thirst after righteousness shall be filled" (Matthew 5:6). This matter of spiritual hunger cannot be overstated. In our journeys to many countries and here in North America we have yet to see a single person have a deep encounter with the Lord without first having a near insatiable thirst for God.

6. You must believe. "Without faith it is impossible to please him: for he that cometh to God must believe that he is, and that he is a rewarder of them that diligently seek him" (Hebrews 11:6).

Like loving, believing is something one does. I am going to believe. I do believe. I have believed. It is a spiritual transaction, and the proof of its accomplishment is spiritual reality.

7. You must share your faith. It is highly impor-

tant to believe that God fills you with love and the Holy Spirit. But there is a world waiting for your love. There are thousands of lost around you.

St. Paul had been filled with the Holy Spirit. And he expressed it this way, "The love of Christ constraineth me..." (II Corinthians 5:14a). Moved and motivated by love, the great missionary plunged on, not driven, but compelled, wishing himself even to be accursed if he might win his lost brethren to Christ.

We can do no less than passionately love the lost. Invite them to Christ. Love your Christian brothers and sisters. Tell them so. And show them by your thoughtful deeds.

Jesus recognized this important principle. First He spoke the healing words. Then to the man with the withered hand He gave the impossible command: Do. "Stretch forth your hand" (Matthew 12:13).

Dr. John Sung, a flame for God in China and the Far East, had a remarkable ministry among Christian believers. One of the keys to it all was the emphasis on doing. Certainly there was fine Bible teaching in his crusades, and great blessing in the churches. But he would not allow them to stop there. They had to share. Go out. Do.

Similarly, the Lay Institutes for Evangelism, conducted by Campus Crusade for Christ all across America and Canada, are distinct and revolutionary because of one key factor—those who attend the seminars and soak up the spiritual atmosphere go out to share their faith door to door. *To do.*

The Rev. D. James Kennedy of the Coral Ridge

Presbyterian Church in Florida was singularly unsuccessful in his effort to teach witnessing to his people—till he began to *do* it with them. The "Evangelism Explosion" that is still unfolding there is contemporary church history in the making.

Doing is not a key to open to us the door of faith. But doing is the nearly forgotten key to the abundant life in Christ.

Finally (and this could be the most important paragraph in the entire book), love is not only a present responsibility. Love must be the continuing response that brings the revolution!

CHAPTER 15
Exploding Love

Exploding Love.

As incongruous as the two words may seem, there is no choice but to place them together. They are a seeming contradiction of terms only because of our inadequate views and cloudy understanding of the nature of divine love.

In an explosion, we are told, there is a rapid multiplication of forces, so rapid as to create extreme violence and a very loud noise. Also, in an explosion there is an expulsive power which sends debris flying in all directions, often disintegrating as it goes.

But the violence and power of an explosion is not only outward. Once the vacuum has been created there is the rush of nature to fill it and the violence of the implosion is, if anything, more extreme than the explosion itself.

Now we will certainly admit that violence and loud noise have little to do with divine love. But God's love does multiply. "Mercy unto you, and peace and love be multiplied" (Jude 2). St. Paul expresses much the same idea, "And this I pray, that your love may abound yet more and more" (Philippians 1:9).

The concepts of love shared in these pages are capable of triggering a spiritual explosion. The expulsion of sin is followed by an inrush of love. If you have seriously considered that love is something you do, that love must be verbalized and expressed, that love must above all be demonstrated by obedience to God, then without doubt the revolution of love will come into your experience. And do not be surprised if love simply explodes.

Love multiplies rapidly. It is a divine and delightful contagion, a heavenly leaven. And when the renewal of the Spirit of God comes to your life and church, yes, there may be only one term to describe it—exploding love.

Gerald McGarvey, a missionary of the Christian and Missionary Alliance in Africa whom we greatly appreciate, has written of an experience we shared at a preachers' conference at Dedougou, Upper Volta. We include it because it illustrates what we have been seeking to say.

"The next morning was something else! After a message on how we are required to love one another if we are to call ourselves Christ's disciples, Mr. Foster asked that all bow their heads. He said, 'You can say that God loves you. You can say that you love God. But can you turn to the one sitting next to you and say you love him? Is there anyone in the room to whom you cannot truthfully say "I love you"?' It was like just before a violent rain when the sky is black but in one hushed moment all you can hear is the far away faint roar of the coming wind. Down on the front row one of the leaders... was weeping. His missionary grasped his hands and they wept together. Then he turned to another missionary and wept on his shoulder.

"It was at that moment that Mr. Foster took my hand and said, 'I love you.' I responded instantly, 'I love you, my brother.' Then he went one way and I the other, taking the hands of our brethren and saying out loud, 'I love you, my brother.' Then it happened. Everyone was out of his seat. We were no longer shaking hands, we were embracing each other. Forgiveness was asked and love was expressed as we shared the moment of divine love together, passing from one to another in what must be called an explosion of love." [1]

And if I may add my observations to Mr. McGarvey's, for about ten minutes we witnessed a manifestation of love and joy, of brokenness and tears that left many of us in awed silence. The overwhelming thought in our minds was, "We have never seen it like this." All praise to the Lord alone!

Now if you will allow me to speculate, I think that love in its purest form is always expanding, abounding—and if the term no longer jars you—exploding.

Jesus expressed the love relationship between Himself and His Father this way, "You gave Me the glory because You loved Me before the world began" (John 17:24, Living Bible). Citing the same scripture, Francis Schaeffer observes, "Among the things we know about the Trinity is that the Trinity was before the creation of everything else and that love existed between the persons of the Trinity

---

[1] Gerald McGarvey, Revival in Dedougou, from *Mali, Upper Volta Tidings*, edited by Ruth Herber (December 1972), p. 8.

before the foundation of the world." [2]

Is it possible that this perfect love in the Trinity has always been an exploding love, that it now is abounding more and more, and that forever divine love goes on multiplying? Our minds boggle at such speculation, but if this immeasurable universe is always rushing outward, it just may be true that God's perfect love is always growing too.

It is certainly not speculative that God is able to manifest Himself most in the lives of those who passionately love Him. "He that hath my commandments, and keepeth them, he it is that loveth me; and he that loveth me shall be loved of my father, and I will love him, and will manifest myself to him" (John 14:21). "I will only reveal Myself to those who love Me, and obey Me" (John 14:23, Living Bible).

Have you ever wondered why it was that Daniel in the Old Testament and John in the New received such great revelations from God? I believe the key was love. Daniel was "greatly beloved," a great lover of God. John was the Apostle of Love, the man who leaned on Jesus' breast because he wanted to.

We are not suggesting here that all who truly love God will necessarily receive end-time visions and apocalyptic revelation. But the Saviour has promised to manifest Himself to those that love Him. And He will do that.

This little book has been written because we believed God wanted it. Moreover, there is an

---

[2] Francis A. Schaeffer, *The God Who Is There*, Hodder and Stoughton, Ltd., London, 1968, p. 97.

assurance in our hearts that the Holy Spirit will use it in many parts of the world to kindle the revolution of love.

Now we have some important words for you, If the revolution of love has come to your heart, thank God. But please do not for a moment feel that this is something which once learned, can be put aside and stored for future reference. Like the manna of old which could not be stored up, this truth is for now, for today, for doing. We do, not to save ourselves nor merit God's favor, but to please Him because we love Him.

Also, please do not ever assume that God's love is exhausted, that its power has been expended. My wife and I pray for you that your love may abound more and more.

Love never fails.

And now you'll understand us when we say, "We love you all."

Other Books by the Author

Books
Believer's Authority
Dam Break in Georgia
Discerning Christian, The
Warfare Weapons

Booklets
Believer's Authority
Fasting: the Delightful Discipline

Books edited with H. Robert Cowles
Holiness Voices
Prayer Voices

Books edited with
H. Robert Cowles and David Jones
Missionary Voices